Planning
for Play

A Developmental
Approach

Gail Bjorklund

Hood College

D1708588

Charles E. Merrill Publishing Company
A Bell & Howell Company
Columbus Toronto London Sydney

Published by
Charles E. Merrill Publishing Company
A Bell & Howell Company
Columbus, Ohio 43216

This book was set in Century Schoolbook.
The Production Editor was Linda Hillis.
The cover was prepared by Will Chenoweth.

*Cover photos, left to right, by Julia Estadt, William Stoll, Values in the
Classroom (Charles E. Merrill, 1977), and William Stoll.*
Photos on pages 7, 10, 12, 26, 29, 32, 34, 38, 51, 56, 57, 68, 74, 76, and
79 by Dixie Lea Smith. Other photos by Gail Bjorklund.

International Standard Book Number: 0-675-08434-2

Library of Congress Catalog Card Number: 77-11236

1 2 3 4 5 6 7 — 83 82 81 80 79 78

Printed in the United States of America

Preface

Play is a part of living. We all play. For children, however, play is especially important. Not only do children spend most of their daily lives involved in play, but play is their way of learning. For these reasons, an understanding of children's play can be an important avenue for adults to learn about the nature of childhood and ways of working with children to optimize their development.

Planning for Play is a multimedia instructional program which examines several aspects of children's play in relation to its role in the child's development. The program consists of four units:

Why do children play?	An introduction to the world of children's play. The major theories of play are examined as a means for describing the special qualities of play and for identifying play behavior in children.
How do children play?	The creative and spontaneous nature of play means that children will approach similar play experiences in many different ways. Systems for describing typical patterns of social and object play are described.
How does play promote development?	The role of play in supporting physical, social, emotional, and intellectual development is covered. A typical day in a nursery school is used to illustrate the variety of learnings inherent in daily play activities.

How can teachers support play?   Alternative approaches to facilitate children's play are presented. Roles such as observing, modeling, and planning are illustrated by specific situations to demonstrate how teachers can effectively build on children's play experiences.

Each of the above units is comprised of three basic components:

1. an introductory cassette/filmstrip (MEDIAPAK).
2. a complementary reading selection in this text.
3. a selection of exercises including observation tasks and discussion questions at the conclusion of each unit.

Students using the *Planning for Play* materials are expected to become actively involved in all aspects of the program by applying learnings to their own experiences in observing and working with young children. The mechanism for such active participation is particularly evident in the exercises. Many of these exercises incorporate actual observations made of children's play in what is called a Play File.

The Play File is a collection of anecdotal records of actual play episodes. The forms provided in the Appendix can be used in making the Play File. Instructors may decide to have each student develop their own individual Play File or groups of students share their observations in a joint file system. Many of the same play incidents will provide appropriate information for several different practice exercises in the text. Therefore, care should be taken to accurately record children's play behavior in the Play File.

Two basic essentials of observation can guide the Play File observations:

1. clear detail.
2. objective accuracy.

Clear detail enables a reader who did not observe the same play episode to gain a full picture of the children's behavior. Developing a good list of descriptive words can be helpful in developing clear detail. For example, while one observer may note that a child "walked" over to the art table, another may record that a child "darted directly to the art table as soon as she entered the room, not even pausing to glance at the materials set up in the table game area or at the hospital props for dramatic play."

A second essential is objective accuracy. It is easy to form personal opinions while observing children. Many opinions are hard to separate from fact. Therefore, care must be exercised to limit personal biases and subjective interpretations. Recording that a child was playing "nicely" means very different things to different people. Does it mean quietly? actively? alone? carefully using the materials? . . . we just don't know.

When actually recording a play session, it is best to select just *one child* on which to concentrate an observation. Record the activities, conversations, and interactions of this child with teachers and other children. For an example of how a play file observation should be done, see the example provided in the Appendix.

In conclusion, it is hoped that those who use the materials of *Planning for Play* enjoy their experiences. Most important, however, is the goal that students find themselves appreciating and supporting children's play more fully.

Acknowledgments

A project such as *Planning for Play,* with its extensive visual component, depends heavily on the support and interest of many individuals. In this regard, I have been most fortunate to have benefited from many very special people.

The impetus for developing this program came from a course in instructional system development offered by John Patrick and James Okey at Indiana University. Their encouragement lead to continued revision with the invaluable guidance of Jerry Brown of the Agency for Instructional Television (AIT) in Bloomington, Indiana, and my graduate advisor in the Interdisciplinary Doctoral Program on Young Children, Sadie Grimmett. Their reviews of Units 2 and 3 contributed greatly to a smoother and more polished final product.

Students both at Indiana University and Hood College offered many helpful suggestions in field testing the materials. I also wish to thank the staff and children of the University Preschool in Bloomington, Indiana for sharing many delightful hours with me and my camera. The preschool programs of Madeline Deckard, Deborah Ziegler, and Beth Reismen were ideal examples of how planning for play really can become operational.

Finally, I wish to thank the children and their parents, as well as the student teachers that I worked with at the Onica Prall Laboratory Preschool at Hood College. In addition to illustrative photographs, they provided many insights into the real dynamics of children's play.

Contents

Unit 1

Why do children play?

Objectives

1. To recognize the major theories of play and the major concepts within each of these theories.
2. To identify the special qualities of play and the types of conditions which best maximize play among children.
3. To describe the values of play for young children.

Components

This unit is composed of five major parts. It is suggested that they be used in the following order:

1. View MEDIAPAK 1, "Why do children play?" and complete the participation questions. Discuss your responses with your classmates or instructor.
2. Read Unit 1 in your text.
3. Select any supplementary reading material from the suggested list (*optional*).
4. Work on the practice exercises at the conclusion of this unit:
    Survey of Preschool Children
    Survey of Parents
    Survey of Teachers
    The Special Qualities of Play (Play File)
    Is It Play? (Play File)
5. Discuss the questions and issues suggested at the end of the unit.

Unit 1

It seems inevitable that an interest in young children's development should also lead to an interest in their play. Children spend much of their time engrossed in play, while adults yearn for the carefree abandon of their own early years so they might return to the world of play. Play seems to have a universal appeal. In many ways, however, we take play for granted. We just naturally expect play to be a part of children's daily routine. Our real understanding of play is only just beginning.

Many questions are being asked about play by parents, teachers, and researchers. We wonder, Why do children play? What, if any, purpose does play serve in children's development? And, finally, if play is important, what are its special qualities? These are the questions to be explored in this unit.

Why Do Children Play?

The motives for play have intrigued scientists, poets, philosophers, educators, psychologists, and parents for decades. The answers proposed by individuals representing a wide spectrum of fields have understandably evolved into a number of often conflic-

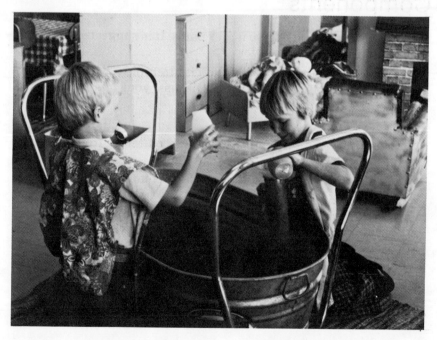

Understanding play helps us to understand children.

ting theories about play. Viewed together, however, they provide the student of young children with enlightening perspectives on why children play.

The following theories of play have been identified in several excellent sources. Among the reviews which are particularly thorough are those of Gilmore (1971), Millar (1968), Ellis (1973), and Mitchell and Mason (1941).

Classical Theories of Play

The classical theories of play first appeared in the late 1800s and after the turn of the century. They shared a concern with explaining the motives and purposes of play toward the goal of understanding why humans play. The rather simplistic approaches of each theory tended to account for only certain aspects of play; yet, the basic concepts within many of these early theories remain in our thoughts about play even today.

- The *surplus energy theory* describes play as a product of excess energy which, when not expended on survival needs, could be released in the form of "aimless" play activity. Children, whose basic needs were satisfied by adults, tended to play in order to release the surplus energy not consumed by work. Anyone who has watched a preschool child can identify examples to support this theory: a child cooped-up indoors on a rainy day, a child listening to a long story during group time. However, not all situations can be explained by this theory.

- The *relaxation theory,* first proposed by Patrick in 1916, takes an opposite view. Play was seen as a means through which energy could be replenished. The active and interesting activities engaged in during play were believed to be more restful and therefore the best remedy for restoring the energy needed for work. Elementary school children who have spent the morning involved in math and language activities illustrate how a short recess period can seem to give them a renewed sense of energy when they return to the classroom.

- The *preexercise* or *practice theory* of Karl Groos suggests that children instinctively play to practice skills they will need during adulthood. The content of play is therefore related to the behavior of the adult world which surrounds children. For

example, children may be seen preparing food and setting the
table in the housekeeping area of a nursery school or making
loud siren noises and arresting speeding tricyclers in the play
yard. The practice theory states that such behaviors are "in-
stinctive" to young children. Our present understanding of
this imitative dramatic play, however, suggests that children
play "mother," "father," and "police officer" roles because
they enjoy behaving like those significant adults they see
around them.

- The *recapitulation theory* sees the motives of play in the past,
  rather than in the future. In play, children "rehearse" the
  activities of their ancestors, thus ridding children of the need
  to express such primitive skills in adulthood, when behaviors
  such as fighting or chasing others would not be considered
  appropriate.

The four major classical theories present an inconsistent picture
of play—each theory seems to contradict the other. All four, however, suggest that instinct is at the root of play behavior. This
belief removes any responsibility for thinking about facilitating
children's play through any type of planning or intervention. In
addition, the concept of play as the opposite of work is a common
theme.

Contemporary Theories of Play

Growing interest in childhood led to theories of play which
reflected a more encompassing and dynamic approach to explaining human behavior. Within these contemporary theories, play is
treated as one aspect of behavior within a more wide-ranging
focus of explaining developmental trends in behavior and causal
relationships between behavior and environment. As a result, the
contemporary theories apply to a greater number of situations
than do the classical theories.

- *Freud's theory of play* presents an extensive system to explain
  children's play. Play was a means to express emotions and to
  master difficult or conflicting events. Using fantasy in play
  allowed children to reenact pleasant memories, to imitate
  adult roles in an attempt to gain a sense of mastery and self-
  esteem, or to play out personal troubles, fears, and emotions in
  a secure atmosphere. In this manner, children would gain a

better understanding of themselves and their world as well as an ability to cope with the realities of living. Examples to support Freud's concepts of play are plentiful. When children start nursery school, the fears of leaving home may prompt a child to bring a favorite toy to school or to comfort a doll in the housekeeping corner by telling it how much fun school really is. In their art work, children may represent their fears by drawing monsters with enormous teeth. The manageable and nonthreatening form of a drawing places the child in control and builds a feeling of mastery over strong emotional forces.

The application of psychoanalytic theory to childrearing and early childhood education tended to place the adult in a passive role. The young child was to be allowed freedom for self-expression, while the parent or teacher observed the child's behavior in an attempt to understand the development

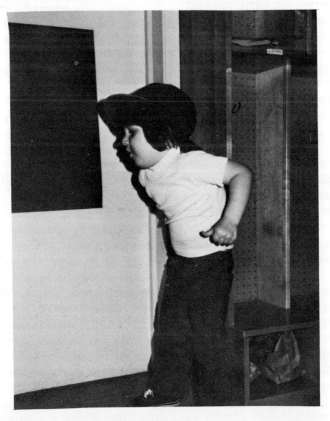

Play is an important means for self-expression!

and needs of the child, rather than to interfere with the play. The critical role of childhood in healthy personality development, and play's important contribution toward this development, may have tended to frighten rather than enlighten those working with young children.

- *Erikson's theory of play* expands upon the pyschoanalytic theory by emphasizing the broader function of play in identity formation. Play became a child's way of learning how to come to terms with reality, to manage life's tasks, and to master skills needed to participate in society. While Freud saw play as an escape from reality into the imaginary world of fantasy, Erikson viewed play as a means of facing reality.

  Erikson stressed the open nature of spontaneous play which enabled the child to adjust play to personal identity needs. During the early years, the developmental needs for independence and initiative would strongly influence the type of play seen among children. Toddlers would tend to use play to practice newly acquired skills, such as walking or talking, in a variety of situations to gain the self-assurance necessary for a sense of independence. Preschool age children, equipped with a basic sense of autonomy, would be inclined to direct play toward initiating creative endeavors. In this way, children would gain a great deal of pleasure and self-worth from imaginative play which allowed them to face reality on their own terms.

  Erikson's views seem to indicate that adults, in addition to observing play in a permissive and noninterfering climate, can assume an active role by adapting experiences to children's capacities in ways that also enable children to actively participate in the daily routines of their world in real and important ways, for example, helping to water the garden or to set the table for a snack. Erikson saw a real danger in separating childhood play from adult work because the division would one day force the child to renounce childhood play in order to learn new behaviors needed for acceptance into the adult world. Therefore, those working with children were urged to provide a rich variety of real experiences in order to add meaning to children's self-expression during spontaneous play.

- *Piaget's theory of play* examines play from the perspective of its contribution to intellectual development. This orientation is important to remember when considering Piaget's concepts on play, for while his theory provides much insight into the world of play, its application may be limited to our understanding of how play contributes to a child's intellectual growth.

According to Piaget, two processes are fundamental to development: assimilation and accommodation. Assimilation represents an effort to change elements from the outside world so they can be incorporated into familiar structures. When a child is given a Frisbee to throw, he may at first try to throw it with the same overhand motion that had worked so well for throwing balls. Accommodation, on the other hand, occurs when the child is called upon to change and adjust to the demands of the outside world when old response structures are no longer adequate. When the old overhand throw just doesn't work for the Frisbee, the child learns a new way to throw it. Piaget believed that more playlike behavior occurred when children were able to assimilate. Using familiar ways of painting is more likely to seem like play than trying to copy new ideas demonstrated by another child.

Piaget's observations of play are categorized into three stages according to the types of assimilative acts children usually performed at different ages: practice play, symbolic play, and games with rules. Thus, as children mature and gain increasing experience with the outside world, the form of their play undergoes qualitative changes. Any type of planning for play must consider these differences in play and how they relate to the child's level of development. In addition, children must be provided an environment which enables them to exert some degree of control over reality in order for the assimilation process to occur. If robbed of this opportunity for play, children will fail to fully develop the thoughts and actions necessary for effective interaction with their environment.

The Special Qualities of Play

The theories of play provide clues to the inherent qualities of play which separate it from other forms of behavior. These play qualities can be examined for their contributions to children's development. Thus, awareness of the qualities of play can be quite helpful in forming a rationale for play: school programs for young

Play is a very special behavior.

children and even parents are often challenged to defend the real value of letting children "just play" when, for example, over half of a child's intelligence is developed by age five (Bloom 1964). Childhood is a period of tremendous learning. It is this very fact that makes play, rather than other, more work-oriented forms of behavior, a valuable medium for learning.

Play Produces a Greater Variety of Behaviors

When children play, the consequences of their actions are minimized. Thus, children feel free and more relaxed to explore their environment. During this exploration, children at play can experiment with a wide variety of behaviors as well as apply variations of a new skill in different contexts. Since a greater number of different forms of behavior are used in play, it is natural that more learning will occur. In addition, children are more likely to try out a variety of behaviors during play and are therefore more likely to explore objects and behaviors which are appropriate to their level of understanding. Observing any toddler playing with a toy will convince you of this valuable aspect of play.

*Observation of sixteen month old
at play*

Kevin, sixteen months old, is playing with a stacking rings toy. At first he shakes the toy vigorously with both hands, laughing as he hears the noise. He removes his hand from the top of the stick and continues shaking. Several of the rings fall off the stick. Kevin momentarily stops shaking the toy and looks at the rings on the floor. As he returns to shaking the rings, he turns the toy upside down, and all the rings fall off the stick. Kevin picks up the largest ring and easily slips it over the stick. He does the same with a smaller ring. He then slowly turns the toy upside down, watching the rings slip off the stick. He tries to get the rings back on the stick by putting the stick through the ring on the floor. He pushes the ring up through the stick but as soon as he lets go, the ring slips down. Kevin then proceeds to return the stick to its upright position and slips all the rings back on the toy.

If Kevin had not been able to manipulate the object freely, think of the rich learning experiences he would have missed.

As a variety of concepts are absorbed through play, the child begins to consolidate and apply experiences. Piaget, in both *Origins of Intelligence in Children* (1952) and *Play, Dreams, and Imitation in Childhood* (1962), identifies the assimilation process as a source of internal motivation. Children who have encountered a rich variety of experiences through play will be equipped with a fuller, more complex understanding of their world and how to function in it.

Play Elicits Creative Responses

Just as the unconstrained character of play promotes variety in behavior, it also enhances the child's capacity to generate novel responses. Playful activity is essentially creative since novel responses are built upon the foundations of early experiences. Play broadens the child's experiences and thus increases the number of creative responses available.

Playing children are creative.

Conditions for enhancing creativity have long been associated with maximizing full human potential. The 1962 yearbook of the Association for Supervision and Curriculum Development (ASCD) suggests the following conditions to enhance creativity. As you examine the list, notice that play can provide many of these conditions.

- encouragement of imagination
- provision for opportunities for choice
- support of cooperative interaction and open communication
- value of new and different ideas
- presentation of real situations for problem solving
- availability of a rich variety of concrete experiences
- development of spontaneity and flexibility

Thus, play serves a valuable function by exercising the child's inherent creative potential.

Research supports this dynamic relationship between play and creativity. Lieberman (1965), for example, attempted to relate creativity, divergent thinking, and playfulness among kindergarteners. She found that ratings of spontaneity, joy, sense of humor, and flexibility were all manifestations of one overall personality trait—playfulness. Playful children were also the more creative, divergent thinkers.

Play Builds Sensitive Awareness

The freedom of play appears to allow more detailed awareness of the environment. Relaxed and unpressured by external demands, children who play are open to the sensory input of the surrounding world. They see, hear, and explore with greater sensitivity. A more varied and detailed picture of objects, events, and people comes from this increased awareness. Children who are aware of more can also do more and learn more while interacting with the environment during play.

Play Allows for Practice of Manageable Behavior Units

Children yearn to cope with life's tasks and master the skills needed to actively participate in the world. During play, the child can break tasks into manageable subunits. These smaller, more fundamental components are repeated over and over in a pattern of practice and refinement. Finally, these subtasks are consolidated and selectively applied to meet the requirements of more complex tasks and situations. The child gains a feeling of success from accomplishing tasks at his own level of functioning.

As adults we often forget the complexity of even everyday situations. Children, so eager to physically participate in their world, use the medium of play to work on fragments of the life they witness. For example, before children can successfully construct a tall building made of blocks, they need to handle the blocks extensively, learn their various properties, bang blocks together to see how they fit, put a few blocks in a pile, knock them down, etc.

Such breakdown of tasks also occurs in social-emotional aspects of development. A child trying to understand the role of parents and various family relationships will reenact family scenes in dramatic play. A two year old or young three may be observed washing dishes or feeding a baby in simple, rather repetitive steps. An older preschooler will have added further subtasks to these routines. Washing dishes, for example, may come at the end of a long eating episode, with more complex progressions of turning on the water, washing with make-believe soap, rinsing, drying with a towel. A child could not move as effectively with such a complex, sequential pattern of play behavior unless subtasks had been mastered individually in earlier play episodes.

Play Builds Self-initiative

Erikson has strongly emphasized the importance of independence and initiative in healthy personality development during the preschool years (Erikson 1950). The child at play is free to make his own decisions. If mistakes are encountered, frustration and feelings of inferiority are minimized because the child is "only playing" and can therefore more freely try other methods or types of play activities. Successful play experiences will increase a child's eagerness and enthusiasm for trying out new ideas.

Play Enhances Humor

It seems important not to forget that play is essentially fun. The frustrations that can easily be associated with directed, academic learning methods are absent from play. The lighthearted, fantasy world of play can place incongruous objects and behaviors together in an atmosphere which is open to the appreciation of humor. The laughter of children enjoying play cannot be matched for its quality of joyfulness. Surely any behavior which brings out such joy in children is to be highly valued.

Identifying Play

The special qualities of play are clearly important aspects of behavior. In order to fully encourage and develop forms of play behavior, the next question of interest becomes, How do you identify play and the types of conditions which seem to maximize playfulness?

Surprisingly, there is no easy answer to the question of identifying play. Members of diverse disciplines have pondered the question in lengthy discussions. As implied in the variety of concepts proposed in the theories of play, there are many and often conflicting views. Part of the problem is that the word *play* is so

Play is fun.

tied up in our everyday vocabulary that we each have our own personal concept of what play really is.

An understanding of play requires first a realization that play is a part of all behavior. Play can occur anywhere and in many different ways. There is no one identifiable subset of behaviors which can exclusively be defined as play. Instead, play becomes a matter of degree or extent on a continuum—behavior can be more or less playlike according to certain criteria.

The following play criteria can provide a useful set of descriptors to identify the degree of playfulness of a situation. Applying these criteria is quite helpful when you realize the special qualities of play and want to assure that a maximum play environment is being provided. If a setting does not provide adequately for play based upon these criteria, then teachers or parents can work toward changing the environment in specific ways to better promote play.

These criteria were first proposed by Eva Neumann (1971) after an extensive analysis of the history and theories of play. Her proposed criteria can be expressed simply by the following questions:

WHO—Who is in control of the play?

WHY—Why is the child motivated to play?

WHAT—What is the content of the play?

Who

This criterion looks at the source of control for play. Children involved in active play will demonstrate greater control over the direction of play. One application of this criterion can be seen in many preschool programs where a major portion of time is devoted to free play—a period during which children select their own play activities.

Obviously, all choices and directions for behavior cannot reside solely with children. The physical properties of the materials children use will limit the type and form of responses. A puzzle, for example, has specific uses and a definite end product, while clay can be used in any number of different ways and therefore tends to produce more playful behavior. The teacher will also exercise some degree of control by deciding to set out certain types of collage materials for the art center, by establishing certain safety limits for the use of carpentry tools, or by verbal interactions with children during play. In addition, during cooperative play other children will share some of the control by deciding who will be the mother and who will be the baby and whether it's time to eat or go to sleep.

Thus, evaluation of play must consider the extent of control given the child as compared to that of some outside agent, such as the play material, a teacher, or another child. To facilitate play, conditions should be provided which limit, as much as possible, the constraints of outside forces upon the child. Children in a play environment should be able to make a greater number of decisions about what and how they will play. Therefore, when you observe play behavior and ask the question, "Who is in control?" you should be able to answer, "The child."

Why

The criterion "Why" is closely related to "Who" in its emphasis on the child. "Why" asks us to examine the motive for the behavior. Play gains its motivation from the child's individual needs and desires. The child plays for the personal satisfaction associated with the processes of play rather than for any rewards associated with an end product.

The internal motivation of play is well illustrated by the approach of young children to art experiences. Children who have not been exposed to external pressures to bring home art projects, for example, will often seem uninterested in the finished product. At the end of the school day, they may even forget which painting is theirs. Yet, observations of these children during their painting or pasting would have indicated an intense concentration and interest in their work.

A child at play is really involved.

External pressure that demands certain forms of behavior can undermine play. A child entering the housekeeping corner who may have come with enthusiastic ideas about "cooking dinner" may feel obligated to change his play if a teacher insists that he will play "hospital" instead.

Because play is internally motivated, it is difficult for us to justify its value for children's development. Children appear to play for no apparent reason. As observers, we fail to understand the satisfactions gained from activity promoted by intangible, internal forces. This internal motivation is strong in children, but can be crushed if a child is continually exposed to demands for specific types of play products or behaviors.

What

   The criterion "What" addresses the content of the play by examining the extent of pretend or make-believe that a child is able to apply to play situations. The content of more playlike behaviors is governed once again by internal concepts of reality: the child as a player is able to "bend" reality to fit personal concepts of reality or imaginary play ideas. This criterion of play emphasizes the importance of symbolic and dramatic forms of activity for young children. Play serves a significant role here, as it enables the child to act out personally meaningful ideas.

   A child at play can, therefore, turn a unit block into a tasty fish to be cooked for dinner or carry on elaborate conversations with a favorite doll. Naturally, some limitations of reality will exist during much of play, but the greater the possibility for children to bring fantasy and imagination to their play, the greater the possibility for play. This is not to say that the child is completely unaware of reality. Play just lets the child put reality aside for the moment to let imagination take over.

Conclusion

   This part of *Planning for Play* has shown that many different answers have been offered to the question, Why do children play? Continued study has led to some of our current ideas about the qualities of play which make it a special behavior in its own right. The importance of the qualities of play should encourage those who are interested in young children to examine the extent of play in the experiences provided for children. Play is many things for children but, above all, play is a child's way of living.

REFERENCES

Bloom, B. *Stability and Change in Human Characteristics.* New York: John Wiley, 1964.

Coombs, A., ed. *Perceiving, Behaving, Becoming.* 1962 Association for Supervision and Curriculum Development Yearbook. Washington, D.C.: Association for Supervision and Curriculum Development, 1962.

Ellis, M. *Why People Play.* Englewood Cliffs, N.J.: Prentice Hall, 1973.

Erikson, E. *Childhood and Society.* New York: W. W. Norton, 1950.

Gilmore, J. B. "Play—A Special Behavior." In Current Research in Motivation, edited by R. N. Haber, pp. 343-55. New York: Holt, Rinehart & Winston, 1966.

Lieberman, J. "Playfulness and Divergent Thinking." *Journal of Genetic Psychology* 107 (1965): 219-24.

Millar, S. *The Psychology of Play.* Baltimore: Pelican Books, 1968.

Mitchell, E. and Mason, B. *The Theory of Play.* New York: A. S. Barnes, 1941.

Neumann, E. "The Elements of Play." Ph.D. dissertation, University of Illinois, 1971.

Piaget, J. *The Origins of Intelligence in Children.* New York: W. W. Norton, 1952.

Piaget, J. *Play, Dreams, and Imitation in Childhood.* New York: W. W. Norton, 1962.

Unit 1
Why do children play?

Survey of Preschool Children

Record the responses of several children to the questions below. Add any additional questions you may wish to ask related to the topic of children's play.

1. What does the word *play* mean to you?

2. What do you do when you play?

3. Do you like to play? Why?

4. What is your favorite thing to do when you play?

5. What are some of the things you do when you are *not* playing?

6. Additional questions:

Unit 1
Why do children play?

Survey of Parents

Record the responses of several parents to the questions below. Add any additional questions you may wish to ask related to the topic of children's play.

1. What words would you use to describe play?

2. Do you think play serves a meaningful function for children? Why? (Why not?)

3. What types of things do you do at home to encourage children's play?

4. How do you feel about preschools which allow children to spend much of their time engaged in play?

5. What kinds of things do you think tend to interfere with children's play?

6. Additional questions:

Unit 1
Why do children play?

Survey of Teachers

Record the responses of several preschool teachers to the questions below. Add any additional questions you may wish to ask or additional comments the teachers may have made.

1. What words would you use to describe play?

2. Do you think play serves a meaningful function for children? Why? (Why not?)

3. What kinds of things do you feel tend to encourage children's play? Interfere with children's play?

   encourage:

   interfere:

4. In what ways do you use play within your preschool program?

5. Additional questions:

22

Why do children play?

The Special Qualities of Play

Gather several observations from your Play File. Analyze these observations for evidence of the special qualities of play listed below.

Play Qualities	Example of Behavior
Spontaneous	
Variety of Behavior	
Creative Responses	
Sensitive Awareness of Environment	
Practice of Manageable Behavior Units	
Self-initiative	
Humor	

Why do children play?

Is It Play?

Select several observations from your Play File and, using the criteria below, analyze the extent of play provided for children. When appropriate, suggest ways play could have been more fully encouraged by the conditions of the environment.

Briefly summarize the play incident:

Evaluate the extent of play according to the following criteria:
  WHO? (Who was in control of the play?)

  WHY? (Was the motivation for the play internal or due to some outside pressure?)

  WHAT? (What is the content of the play and is the reality of this content determined by the child?)

How could this play have been further extended? Name some specific ways that conditions could have been changed to more fully encourage play.

Why do children play?

Discussion Questions

1. There is a tendency to classify play as the opposite of work. Why do you feel this tendency has developed? In what ways can such a practice interfere with the development of realistic play expectations for children?

2. When examining the criteria and special qualities of play to determine the extent of play among children, it is clear that all children do not experience play. What might be several factors which would tend to interfere with children's play development?

Unit 2

How do children play?

Objectives

1. To recognize the variety of ways children approach play situations.
2. To identify levels of social interactions among children during their spontaneous play.
3. To identify types of object play according to levels of practice play, symbolic play, and games with rules.
4. To select play materials and activities which facilitate a variety of play processes and are appropriate for the child's developmental level and experience.

Components

This unit is composed of five major parts. It is suggested that they be used in the following order:

1. View MEDIAPAK 2, "How do children play?" and complete the participation questions. Discuss your responses with your classmates or instructor.

2. Read Unit 2 in your text.

3. Select any supplementary reading material from the suggested list (*optional*).

4. Work on the practice exercises at the conclusion of this unit:

    Observing Levels of Social Play (Play File)
    Observing Levels of Object Play (Play File)
    Looking at the Play Potential of Toys

5. Discuss the questions and issues suggested at the end of the unit.

The spontaneous nature of young children's play is reflected in the many ways children approach their play. Thus, when asking the question, "How do children play?" observers are confronted with the elusive task of describing processes which are by their very nature unique and individual.

Continued study of children's play has, however, led to the development of methods for describing certain stages of play without destroying play's unique essence. Such descriptions of how children play help us to better understand the nature and purposes of play.

Observations of typical play scenes can almost always be described by two basic forms of play:

- social play: how children relate to one another during play
- object play: how children use physical materials in their play

Since social and object interactions with the environment are major influences upon human development, identifying these two forms of play at their various levels can be useful ways to both assess and stimulate development. Social and object play opportunities are fundamental mediums for learning. Therefore, methods for classifying both social and object play can be helpful in identifying a child's stage of play. Stages of social and object play allow for classification of behavior in ways that others can comprehend. A child's performance can be evaluated in accordance with developmental norms for progression through the various levels of social and object play.

Since play is spontaneous, it is important to realize that a wide range of behaviors will fit within each category. In addition, not all children will follow the specific age-related trends described for levels of social and object play. Prior to examining the specific stages within social and object play, it is important to recognize several additional assumptions underlying the play processes involved.

Assumptions Underlying Play Processes

The assumptions which form the basis for describing patterns of play processes are general concepts which pervade all play behaviors. It is important to understand these assumptions before categorizing a child's social or object play into certain stages.

*Most play involves both social and object
forms of interaction.*

Often, we can conclude too quickly that a child is in, for example,
the parallel stage of social play. Before we can begin making such
classifications we must first realize the subtle, complex factors
involved in making this determination. Let's examine the assumptions underlying play processes.

Play Processes Are Unique

Play, in its best and purest form, springs from within the child.
Each child brings to play interests, needs, and abilities that are
highly personal. Thus, each child will use play materials in ways
that are unique and individual. Not only will individual children
differ among themselves, but even the same child will from day to
day and from moment to moment try out new approaches to play.

We can learn a great deal about children by observing how they
play. Children reveal not only their interests and abilities but also
their fears and misunderstandings through play. Sensitive awareness of patterns that are revealed in play can give us clues as to
ways of relating to children and of supporting play more effectively.

Play Processes Are Developmental

Similar to other areas of development, play processes follow a
series of developmental stages. As a result, certain patterns are
revealed which follow general, age-related trends.

Factors that cause these changes to occur can be related to two
fundamental forces: maturation and experience. Maturation involves the natural unfolding of innate characteristics over time.
Children will demonstrate new play behaviors simply because
they are older and have attained a higher level of performance
with maturity. We have little control over the course of matura-
tional forces. For example, in the domain of physical maturation,
preschoolers of five years of age will be able to engage in outdoor
climbing play with greater skill and self-assurance than younger
three year olds simply because their bones and muscles have
grown and strengthened.

Experience is a second force in influencing development. Physical manipulation of materials in the environment as well as
social interactions will greatly affect the quality of a child's play.
The child with a rich variety of play experiences will progress
smoothly through the sequential levels of play. The child who,
over the years, has had the opportunity to climb, from simple, low
climbers to more advanced jungle gym apparatus, will progress
through various stages of ability more effectively than the child
who has not had exposure to actual climbing experiences.

Knowledge of the developmental nature of play enables teachers and parents to have more realistic expectations of children. It
is more likely that play materials will be offered and social play
experiences provided which are appropriate to the child's matura-
tional level and level of past experiences.

Play Processes Are Hierarchial

Most behavior that follows developmental stages also tends to
be hierarchial. Each stage builds upon another, with earlier
stages providing valuable foundations for achievements at higher
levels. For those concerned with play this means that the importance of the early stages of play must be realized and fostered to
the fullest.

It is important to understand that stage-oriented categories
serve to organize and describe characteristic patterns of behavior.
The stages themselves are not separate and distinct; rather, they
flow in a continuous fashion with few identifiable points of begin-

ning or ending. Children will also vary within the stages. Thus, a child may use easel paint in a more advanced, symbolic manner, drawing representational pictures and naming them appropriately. When using clay, the same child may still be using earlier sensory explorations only.

Describing Social Play

Children's play can be categorized according to its quality of social interaction with other children. Every play situation involves some form of association (or nonassociation) with other children. These levels of social interaction tell us something about the general pattern of a child's behavior.

Mildred Parten's early study of social participation among preschool children marked the beginning of what has become a classic way of viewing levels of social play (Parten 1932). Her systematic observations of actual play formed the basis for developing the following levels of social play:

Solitary Play. Play that occurs without reference to other children. Even when other children may be nearby, the child engaged in solitary play will continue her play as if no one were there. Generally, solitary play occurs when the child is alone. However, young toddlers who, for example, are playing near other children may push another child roughly aside without seeming to recognize that the other child was anything more than an object. This latter situation can also be termed solitary play, for although the child may not strictly be "alone," the child plays as if she were since other children are not recognized.

Onlooker Play. Play that includes passive observation of the activity of peers without actual participation in the play observed. The onlooking child will often continue with her own play, occasionally looking at the activity of others. This onlooking form of social participation can be a rich source of learning for the child inexperienced in higher levels of social play or the child who may not know the other children. These observations can provide valuable information regarding appropriate models of social interaction.

Parallel Play. Play of a companionate nature, with similar materials and in close proximity, but with no personal interaction. A child engrossed in parallel play will often glance at the work of an adjacent child, but will return to her own activity. This form of social interaction is often a child's introduction to social concepts such as sharing and taking turns. The fact that children are involved in similar activities also makes children more aware of their common interests and abilities. At the art table or when playing table games children consistently tend to demonstrate this type of social play.

Playing with dolls can be a good way to make a friend.

Associate Play. Play among two or more children that is loosely organized around a common activity, shared interests, or play materials. Unlike parallel play, associative play implies beginning levels of social interaction. These interactions may not last long, but the exchanges are evidence of definite awareness and association among the children involved. For example, children who are engaged in associative play will demonstrate appropriate speech patterns when responding to other children. They may also begin to share dramatic play roles. The themes and roles may shift direction during this dramatic play, but the play sequence will continue.

Cooperative Play. Play among two or more children with common goals and complementary roles, of relatively long duration and complexity. When a child leaves the play group, the play disintegrates since it has been built around cooperative interaction with other children. Often, specific rules may govern the nature of cooperation expected among participating children. This type of social play demonstrates not only children's awareness of others but also their sensitivity to beginning levels of social rules.

This system for describing social play tends to follow a consistent pattern of stage progressions. Young infants and toddlers most often play in ways that can be described as solitary and onlooker. As children grow older and increase their exposure to a wider variety of social play opportunities, parallel play may also become common. By age three or four, the associative level of social participation will become more and more evident. Not until children have developed sufficient language ability and prior social experience, usually around age five, will they consistently demonstrate preferences and competences for the cooperative level of social play.

Stage Levels of Social Play

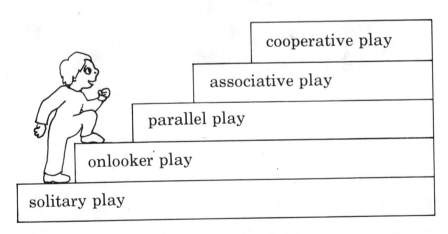

cooperative play

associative play

parallel play

onlooker play

solitary play

Because social play has a hierarchial and developmental nature, examples of all levels of social play can be seen in children's play, particularly that of older preschoolers. Thus, a five year old child who may usually play in cooperative play endeavors with her friends will also enjoy solitary play situations. A child will

generally move in and out of several levels quite easily. For example, John may begin his play at the art table beside two other
children. Observing the play of some other children in the block
area, John may decide to join their play after finishing his art
activity. While playing with the blocks he may join the other
children in building a boat which the group of children jointly
decide will be used to fish for whales.

Children need opportunities for all levels of
social interactions.

Children need experiences with all levels of social interactions
Preschool programs are excellent environments for these social
play experiences since a great number of children are consistently
available. Preschool teachers must try to incorporate varied forms
of social play within the daily play program at levels appropriate
to the developmental needs of each child. Therefore, materials
should be available which can be used in varied forms of social
play—table games for solitary or parallel play, housekeeping materials such as dishes and dress-ups for group play, or two trucks
which can be shared in cooperative play. Children should be
allowed to experience social interaction at their own pace; a young
three should be allowed to spend plenty of time in solitary or

onlooker play before being expected to move into more interactive forms of social play.

Describing Object Play

An additional way of looking at how children play is to examine children's use of play materials. Most play depends on the support of play materials such as toys.

Piaget offers many insights into children's use of objects in his examination of the development of thought structures revealed in ongoing play behavior (Piaget 1962). Play is viewed in Piaget's theory as a special behavioral category called assimilation. As assimilation, play represents a way of taking the outside world and manipulating it so the environment (play objects) fits the child's existing way of structuring and viewing the world. These assimilative acts can be readily applied to children's use of play materials in what we will term *object play*.

As Piaget observed children at play, he identified three characteristic types of play which distinguished children's various patterns of approaches to the use of play objects. These three types of object play are as follows:

Practice Play. Play where objects are used in an exploratory, sensorimotor nature as actions are repeated over and over again. A child who is playing with blocks might first hold them and feel their shapes and forms. Then she might place them in a variety of positions, balancing them carefully. Finally, she knocks them over and starts to build with them once again. Through practice play the child develops and consolidates present ways of interacting with objects in the environment. However, practice play behaviors are not exercised with the goal of practice, but rather for the sheer joy of using one's new powers.

Symbolic Play. Play utilizing symbolic representation to integrate its elements. Imaginative make-believe characterizes symbolic play and is seen in many aspects of preschool play behavior: in sociodramatic play scenes where children pretend they are family members, doctors, police officers; in verbal descriptions where objects are given new qualities to represent absent objects, such as when an empty box is called a car and is pushed around the floor. This type of object play requires children to project their mental images upon objects in ways that can change the characteristics of the objects and enable them to represent different forms.

Games with Rules. Play where social reality, rather than make-believe, governs or regulates the action. This last form of object play rarely occurs before age four and is most characteristic of play among seven to eleven year olds. The increased socialization among children by the older preschool years begins to necessitate the use of rules to regulate play. Children formulate rules to govern their use of objects through a code handed down from earlier generations or by temporary agreement. Among preschool children, the rules are in the latter category and therefore are very simple and can change to fit different situations. For example, a child playing with blocks may decide that a structure must be built in a certain way and will become very upset if someone interferes with these "rules." An element of competition often enters into games with rules. This may begin with simple games like jumping from stairs; the point of the game is to see who can jump the farthest, and anyone who falls is not counted.

Children use objects in symbolic play.

The developmental and hierarchial nature of these types of object play means that practice play is the primary type of play in which infants and toddlers engage. With the onset of advanced language forms, symbolic play increases, becoming especially characteristic of the preschool age child. Games with rules do not form a major component of children's play until the end of the preschool years, reaching a peak by the fourth or fifth grade. Nevertheless, all types of play can be identified in some degree among children of all ages. Like social play interactions, object play opportunities need to be varied so children can gain experience in all forms of object play.

New materials are explored in practice play.

Similarly, when children are confronted with unfamiliar objects, it is not unusual to witness a return to a practice play level, using sensorimotor exploration. This type of play enables the child to understand what the object is like and the various ways it can be used. Following adequate practice play behaviors, the child may begin to demonstrate symbolic play with the material or attribute certain rules to the object's use. It is important to allow children the time to work through these developmental stages of object play since children will vary in the experience levels they bring to various play objects.

Shared Qualities of Social and Object Play

Observations of social and object play have indicated that certain levels of social play tend to be accompanied by certain levels of object play. For example, since practice play, by nature, is an investigative activity, it is most commonly observed with solitary or parallel social interactions. Symbolic play, while it can occur in solitary play, is more likely to be seen in associative or cooperative forms of social play. Similarly, games with rules can be encouraged by cooperative forms of interactions where rules can be helpful in establishing patterns for social interaction. Children who have skills in cooperative forms of social play may be more likely to use objects symbolically or with games with rules.

It is helpful to consider the interrelationships between social and object play when planning for play. The types of objects made available for play can influence the patterns of social and object interactions among children. Certain materials, like dramatic play props, can promote associative or cooperative play as well as symbolic play. In an attempt to facilitate all levels of social and object play, teachers need to be certain that a balanced variety of play materials is available. In addition, teachers need to know which stages of play children may be moving into in order to help these children in the development of new social and object play skills.

Some materials can help children play with one another.

The chart below illustrates some of the typical ways common nursery school materials may be used by children. You may think of some additional ways each material could be used in other types of social and object play. It is not unusual to have a material that can be played with by children in *all* stages of social and object play.

SOME TYPICAL WAYS MATERIALS ARE USED IN PLAY

	Practice	Symbolic	Games with Rules
puzzles	✓		
ball	✓		✓ *
unit blocks	✓	✓	
rocking boat		✓	
set of dishes		✓	
dress-ups		✓	
pegboards	✓		
easel paints	✓	✓	
puppets		✓	
clay	✓		
trucks		✓	
grocery store		✓	
sandbox	✓		

*older children

	Solitary	Onlooker	Parallel	Assoc	Coop
puzzles	✓		✓		
ball				✓	✓
unit blocks	✓	✓	✓	✓	✓
rocking boat				✓	
set of dishes				✓	✓
dress-ups				✓	✓
pegboards	✓		✓		
easel paints	✓				
puppets			✓	✓	
clay	✓	✓	✓		
trucks		✓	✓	✓	
grocery store				✓	✓
sandbox	✓	✓	✓		

Unit 2

Conclusion

Attempts at unraveling and understanding the patterns of human behavior are not easy tasks. When trying to discover how children play the task becomes especially difficult since play is such a unique and individualized activity. From the miriad of play behaviors, two major ways to describe play in social and object domains can be applied to planning for play.

Knowledge of social and object patterns of play among the children with whom one is working can help in identification of differences among the children as well as reasons underlying some of these differences. Since play follows developmental trends, children who consistently demonstrate levels of play unusual for their age can be identified and more carefully observed to detect potential reasons for their play behavior patterns. Additional play experiences and needed support from teachers can then be offered to help these children move into other levels of social and/or object play.

REFERENCES

Parten, M. "Social Participation among Preschool Children." *Journal of Abnormal and Social Psychology* 33 (1932): 243-69.

Piaget, J. *Play, Dreams, and Imitation in Childhood.* New York: W. W. Norton, 1962.

Observing Levels of Social Play

Gather several observations from the Play File of children of
varying ages. Individually, or in small groups, discuss the patterns of social play that emerge as you use the following chart to
help you sort out the observations.

Age	Examples of Social Play (briefly describe children's behavior)	sol	onl	par	asc	coop
2						
3						
4						
5						
6						

1. Which types of social play seem to be most characteristic of the
   ages you observed?
2. How did the materials the children were using in the examples
   contribute to their levels of social play?
3. Compare the levels of one type of social play across ages. What
   differences or similarities do you notice, for example, between
   parallel play among two year olds and that of five year olds?

How do children play?

Observing Levels of Object Play

Gather several observations from the Play File of children of varying ages. Use the chart below to help you sort out and organize your observations.

Age	Materials Used	How the Children Played with the Materials	Level of Object Play		
			pract	symbol	rules
2					
3					
4					
5					
6					

Compare the differences and similarities that have emerged in the uses of play materials among children (1) of the same age and (2) of different ages.

Unit 2
How do children play?

Looking at the Play Potential of Toys

Using the toys pictured in the Appendix, or actual samples of play materials from a preschool, thing about the ways children might use the materials during their play.

Describe or name the material:

List the variety of ways the toy could be used by children during play:

Arrange the play ideas you have listed above according to the type of object play which best characterizes the activity:

Practice Play:

Symbolic Play:

Games with Rules:

How do children play?

Looking at the Play Potential of Toys (cont.)

Describe some typical ways children of different ages might use the material during their play:

Age	Examples of Typical Types of Play	Level of Object Play
2		
3		
4		
5		
6		

Unit 2
How do children play?

Discussion Questions

1. Which toys or materials seem to lend themselves to one particular type of social or object play, regardless of the child's age? Why?

2. Are there some materials which are used in all play processes of social and object play, and by children of all ages? What qualities do these materials seem to share?

3. Compare the positive and negative aspects of materials which:
   a. elicit one level of play only.
   b. are appropriate for all levels of social and/or object play.
   c. are useful for only a selected age range of children.
   d. are useful across ages.

4. What play materials would you provide for six children between the ages of three and five who were members of your play group? (*List at least ten.*)

Unit 3

How does play promote development?

Objectives

1. To identify the values of play in physical, social, emotional, and intellectual areas of development.
2. To justify the choices of play materials and activities based on their developmental values for children.

Components

This unit is composed of five major parts. It is suggested that they be used in the following order:

1. View MEDIAPAK 3, "How does play promote development?" and complete the participation questions. Discuss your responses with your classmates or instructor.
2. Read Unit 3 in your text.
3. Select any supplementary reading material of interest from the suggested list (*optional*).
4. Work on the practice exercises at the conclusion of this unit:

   Developmental Analysis of Play Materials
   Sampling the Values of Play (Play File)
   Analysis of a Plan for Play
5. Discuss the questions and issues suggested at the end of the unit.

Speculations about the values and purposes of play are not new. Since ancient times, philosophers have pondered the question, "Why do people play?" Many types of answers have emerged. The recent revival of interest in play has definitely added new perspectives to our views of play and its importance for people, especially for children.

Play is increasingly recognized as a special behavioral process which provides opportunities that are essential to human development. As our society acts upon and expands its goal of optimizing the development of all young children, it becomes necessary for society to look to play as a mechanism for promoting development.

Play in Early Childhood Education

The field of early childhood education has played a particularly important role in establishing the values of play for children. Traditionally, nursery school programs have centered around spontaneous play experiences. The post-Sputnik era challenged what had become an accepted "play-way" approach. Concern with compensatory education for the economically and culturally deprived led to an emphasis on the acquisition of academic skills. Notions of Bloom (1964) and Hunt (1960) regarding the stimulation of development by enriching the environment during the early years gained wide acceptance. Their concepts provided the rationale for many intervention programs for young children which took an academic, skill-oriented view of early childhood education.

Soon even middle class parents who had formerly provided unquestioning support of play in nursery school programs were wondering why Johnny couldn't read after spending a few months in nursery school.

This chain of events prompted many early childhood professionals to clarify their convictions and practices regarding play. Leaders such as Milly Almy sought to match the results of actual experiences with children with the concepts of leading developmental theories, notably those of Freud, Erikson, and Piaget (Almy 1966). This method of counterattack provided a model which helped educators identify the function of play in terms of its role in promoting the child's development.

Play for Development's Sake

Relating play to the developmental needs of children is a particularly appropriate approach for teachers of young children. It enables teachers to justify play when responding to parents concerned about their child's success in school as well as professional advocates of academic preschool models.

The value of play as a learning medium can be explained in terms of all aspects of development—physical, social, emotional, and intellectual. Each aspect of development, and play's way of promoting its growth, will be discussed separately. It is important to remember, however, that play does not promote one area of development apart from another: the same play experience can effectively promote all aspects of growth simultaneously. Separating each developmental area for the purpose of discussion can provide a clearer picture of the special ways we can plan for play to touch on all aspects of growth.

Play Promotes Physical Development

Physical development is promoted by active use of the body. Children at play are almost continually involved in motion; thus, on even a very simple level, physical skills grow through play. Physical development is usually broken down into two types of motor skills—gross and fine.

Gross motor skills involve the use of large muscles through locomotor activities such as climbing, running, balancing, and pulling. Children seem to involve their whole bodies as they engage in gross motor play. Outdoor play such as swinging, climbing on jungle gyms, riding tricycles, or moving on pieces of equipment clearly demonstrates how play builds gross motor skills and enhances children's coordination.

Fine motor skills are those which allow children to coordinate hand and eye movements through activities such as cutting and pasting, working puzzles and table games, painting, or pouring water in and out of containers. As children engage in this fine motor play, motor precision also grows through direct manipulation of materials.

Both types of physical skills are built through persistent and repetitive action. Play is well suited for this practice-type activity

Physical skills grow through play.

since it allows children to continue their activity in pleasurable, not drill-like, circumstances. Therefore, materials which require physical involvement must be available over time so children can continue to practice and master these skills. Various levels of difficulty should always be available; children who attempt more challenging physical tasks will also gain satisfaction and confidence from being able to return to a task they know they can master.

The payoffs of physical mastery of the body and objects in the environment are many. Of particular significance is the sense of self-confidence and autonomy a child gains from the ability to demonstrate a newly learned task. In addition to feelings of personal well-being, motor activity promotes physical health. Only through active use will the body grow and develop properly. A healthy physical structure will in turn support continued success at physical tasks so important in childhood. Disease and sickness are also more easily resisted by a healthy, physically fit body. Since health is directly related to all aspects of development, it is therefore a key concern of parents and teachers. Clearly, play serves a vital function in developing the skills and health important to physical development of young children.

Play Provides for Social Development

All play activities inevitably provide a chance for some level of social participation. Play enables children to gradually build their awareness of others as well as their understanding of themselves as individuals within a group. Thus, as children move into more interactive stages of social play, they begin to share what they have learned about themselves and others.

As children join in the use of play materials, they experience directly the demands of social reality. Through interaction with other children and continued support and guidance of adults, children gain skills in social living. Awareness of others' rights and property, the ability to settle disputes in acceptable ways, the fun of sharing a pleasurable activity, laughing over a joke—all are experienced as children play with one another. These firsthand experiences provide a foundation for socialization that lecture methods or verbal discussions of social rules just cannot provide.

The process of socialization comes slowly for children and is built from continued and repeated experiences. Conceptually, children are only just beginning to form an awareness of others as

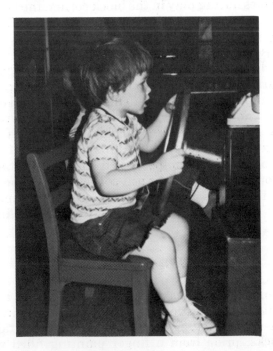

Children grow socially through dramatic play.

separate from themselves. This may often make it hard for children to understand the feelings and reactions of other children or see things from their point of view. Once again the combination of maturation and actual social interactions will provide the basis for such social learnings. Teachers who are sensitive to the level of social development of children will not place unrealistic demands on children to share materials or to join a group. Spontaneous play gives teachers a chance to observe a child's level of social competence in natural situations. Armed with such understanding, the teacher can then use play situations to provide activities and materials which build on a child's present needs and abilities. For example, a child with little understanding of how to join in a group of others at play can be encouraged to enter the housekeeping area if enough props are available for several children to join in similar types of play. Perhaps a hospital scene has been enacted and an extra uniform will make the child feel more a part of the group.

An additional aspect of social play concerns the child's sense of identity and self-awareness. One way play can build on this aspect of development is through sociodramatic play. As children try out new roles during play in the block corner, the housekeeping area, or on the playground, they learn to understand the qualities of roles they see around them—mother, father, baby, firefighter, nurse, etc. By actually trying out these roles in make-believe play the child can experiment with many different types of behaviors and learn which are most comfortable for him. The quiet child, for example, can donn a whistle and badge and emerge as a police officer who can command others to stop at the traffic light. Through the lighthearted spirit of play, the child is free to test out new behaviors to best fit within his personal self-image. The reactions of both adults and peers to a child's activities will also provide important feedback for self-concept formation. The child whose play facilitates positive experiences and supportive encouragement will emerge from play with strong feelings of self-awareness.

Play Expresses Emotional Development

A wide range of emotions arise in play—joy from a satisfying music experience, frustration from having to wait in turn for a tricycle, anger from having someone knock down a tall building made of blocks, pride from a finger painting filled with many designs and colors.

The value of play as a vehicle for emotional expression has been well documented by play therapists such as Virginia Axline (1969). Emotional self-expression seems to be especially facilitated during the use of creative, open-ended play in dramatic play, painting, block building, or sand and water play.

Emotional development involves three phases: (1) identifying feelings, (2) accepting feelings, and (3) expressing feelings. During play, children have many opportunities to experience directly a wide variety of feelings in themselves and in others. Children gradually learn what kinds of behaviors accompany certain actions and feelings, and through the help of adults, learn words that identify various emotional states.

Play environments which allow children to experience emotions and discuss them when they occur will facilitate acceptance of emotions. Acceptance of emotions is an important forerunner to finding appropriate ways for expressing emotions. Strong feelings like anger can be most effectively dealt with in their real states as they occur spontaneously in play. Children can act out their anger in the protection of fantasy or through a vehicle such as clay or woodworking.

Emotions may be shown as children wait for a turn.

Play offers an additional opportunity for emotional growth by enabling children to carry out their own ideas. The competence and sense of mastery that grow from such self-control have been linked to healthy personality development by researchers like Robert White (1960). Erikson (1963) has also identified the importance of children's senses of autonomy and initiative in building emotional well-being. Children who acquire feelings of self-esteem through positive interactions with their environment will tend to develop sound emotional foundations.

During play the child is able to exert control over his actions as well as form the motives for action from within himself. These are two essential qualities of processes such as competence, autonomy, and initiative that are linked so closely with emotional development. Much self-awareness will grow in children who can express their emotions and ideas and who can practice needed skills through play situations.

Play Fosters Intellectual Development

The cognitive aspects of play have received particular attention in response to pressures to justify the learning potential of play. Piaget's theories have helped establish the special function that play serves toward intellectual development. He argues for the importance of direct interaction with the environment and for experiences where the child is able to fit reality into his own way of thinking through the process Piaget calls assimilation. Play provides an ideal setting for both interactions with the environment and assimilation.

Play enables the child to integrate and organize learnings acquired by actual sensorimotor or concrete experiences within his present thought structures. As children directly manipulate materials, they can fit new concepts within their existing way of viewing the world and how it works. For example, during water play, funnels and tubes may be introduced to help transfer water from various sizes of containers. As children use the materials, concepts of volume and quantity, gravity and pressure are experienced in ways that will later facilitate understanding of these concepts in more abstract ways.

Within the basic processes and structures of intellectual development, specific areas can be identified which reflect intellectual growth. Among the more important areas in terms of play's role in promoting intellectual development are the following:

- language development
- perceptual skills
- creative thought processes

Children's abilities in each of these areas will enable them to gain an understanding of their world through the acquisition of knowledge and the building of cause and effect relationships.

Language development involves both communicating with others and understanding the concepts underlying words, the tools of language. Research in language development has demonstrated that children who have had a rich variety of experiences and contact with their cultural world will have better language skills. By adding stimulating new materials to play, children will be able to form the mental symbols of the words needed for language comprehension.

Play is also a fertile ground for verbal aspects of language development. Children at play can converse freely with one another about ideas that have strong personal meaning. Adults who join in these conversations and elaborate upon the children's ideas can enhance children's language abilities.

Perceptual skills help children process and organize sensory input. The first aspect of perceptual development is the provision for adequate and varied sensory stimulation. Play materials provide an excellent means of developing the senses of sight, hearing, and touch. As children use materials during play, they coordinate all the sensory input they can acquire and use their perceptions to develop meaningful and appropriate responses. Watching children at play we see them engaging their whole bodies in active exploration, using every sense to acquire information. As an example, during block play children identify various shapes and sizes by touching and holding the blocks, by looking at them from several directions, by moving the blocks into a variety of positions and watching the results, and by listening to the blocks as they tumble to the floor. Visual, auditory, tactile, and kinetic senses of motion and body movement are used during play interactions. All areas of perceptual development are important, for it is through the senses that children will experience their environment.

Creative thought processes are a channel for curiosity and imagination. As children produce several alternative responses to a situation, they are acquiring skills and attitudes which will expand rather than narrow their future learning. Problem solving is best fostered by an open "let's find out" attitude. Raw materials

Size relationships are experienced during play.

such as paint, clay, blocks, or water, which by their very nature warrant experimentation and imaginative usage, are excellent tools for stimulating creative self-expression. Situations which allow only one response discourage children's initiative and sense of curiosity. Not only is creativity hampered, but zest for learning and discovery can be crushed. Playful encounters can provide excellent conditions for creative thought because the child is more fully able to utilize imaginative powers which seem to abound in young children.

All the above areas of intellectual growth share important qualities—direct experience and active involvement. Preschool intellect is tied to concrete, firsthand experiences. Obviously, play provides many opportunities for this type of intellectual growth.

Play Materials and Development

The materials available for play essentially become the tools through which all areas of development are promoted. As we examine common materials of play, it should become increasingly evident that each material and each activity touch upon *all* aspects of development.

For example, blocks provide for *physical development* on a gross motor level as children lift, pull, climb over, and balance on them. Fine motor skills are practiced in the building of structures that use smaller unit or table-sized blocks. Blocks can attract *social participation* among children. During play, children confront the demands of others who are using similar or nearby materials as well as experience the fun of working jointly on building efforts. Role playing often results when building fire stations, hideouts, and space stations. *Emotional development* comes when anger is expressed toward the child who knocks down another's work. After long periods of planning and hard effort, joy and satisfaction are felt from the sense of mastery and competence which grows from active endeavor. *Intellectual development* enters as children notice size relationships, classify according to shape while building a tower, compare weights while lifting and pulling blocks, and create imaginative designs with the materials. The conversations that surround block play not only engage children in social interactions but also give them opportunities for language development.

Many play materials have potential for all areas of growth.

By recognizing the variety of developmental achievements that occur spontaneously during play, you can appreciate the value of play more fully. In addition, those who recognize the potential for learning in the materials they offer to children will be more likely to build upon these learnings when they occur in play. An abundance of play materials is not essential. What is needed is a balanced variety of materials which touch upon all areas of development. Children's development can be promoted in all four areas regardless of what activity they select during play.

Play for Fun's Sake

While the value of play in terms of development and learning is important, the value of play as fun should not be denied. We all want to maximize the learning in the early years, but never at the risk of sacrificing fun. Childhood is a time of life for the carefree abandon of play, never to be experienced so fully again. Fun, laughter, pleasure, and joy are important components of a healthy personality which need to be fostered during the early years just as much as physical, social, emotional, and intellectual growth.

Many people have long believed that when we are involved in activities which we initiate and enjoy, we not only learn more, but we maintain a healthier self-image and general outlook on life. Research seems to support such a notion. For example, in a study of children reared in an institution (Rheingold 1956), the lack of pleasure which children could derive from playful interactions with adults and other children contributed to below normal developmental progress. On the other hand, three and five year old children who were given an opportunity to play with materials in a problem-solving game prior to testing did just as well in solving the problem as children who were shown how to solve the problem by an adult (Sylva 1976). More importantly, the children who were allowed to play showed greater perserverance, organization, and enthusiasm toward the task. Environments which operate in a funlike atmosphere do seem to enhance learning.

Therefore, when planning for play experiences that are rich in their potential for physical, social, emotional, and intellectual development, teachers and parents should also consider whether or not children will enjoy the experience. Justifications which show how children are learning and growing in various areas of development are surely helpful in providing a rationale for play; however, it can be easy to lose sight of the fundamental value of fun in our concern for enhancing development. We need not be ashamed to admit the fun value of play by using such phrases as "play is the work of children" or "play is children's business." Such phrases often undermine play by trying to equate it with more serious concerns of an achievement, work-oriented society. Play should always be playful.

Conclusion

The early years are filled with rapid growth in all aspects of children's development. A desire to enhance development contributes to an interest in providing a rich variety of learning opportunities for children to promote physical, social, emotional, and intellectual growth. For young children, play is the most appropriate medium to present such learning opportunities. Adults who are aware of the potential of play experiences for developmental growth can more effectively build on the spontaneous learnings of play.

REFERENCES

Almy, M. "Spontaneous Play: An Avenue for Intellectual Development." *Young Children* 22 (1968): 265-77.

Axline, V. *Play Therapy*. New York: Ballentine Books, 1969.

Bloom, B., *Stability and Change in Human Characteristics*. New York: John Wiley, 1964.

Erikson, E. *Childhood and Society,* 2nd. ed. New York: W. W. Norton, 1963.

Hunt, J. McV. *Intelligence and Experience*. New York: Ronald Press, 1960.

Piaget, J. *Origins of Intelligence in Children*. New York: W. W. Norton, 1952.

Piaget, J. *Play, Dreams, and Imitation in Childhood*. New York: W. W. Norton, 1963.

Rheingold, H. "The Modification of Social Responsiveness in Institutional Babies." *Monographs of the Society for Research in Child Development* 1956, 21, (2).

Sylva, K. "The Role of Play in the Problem-Solving of Children 3-5 Years Old." In *Play: Its Role in Development and Evolution,* edited by J. Bruner, A. Jolly, and K. Sylva, pp. 244-57. New York: Basic Books, 1976.

Tyler, B. "Play." In *Curriculum for the Preschool-Primary Child,* edited by C. Seefeldt, pp. 225-46. Columbus, Ohio: Charles E. Merrill Publishing Co., 1975.

White, R. "Competence and the Psychological Stages of Development." In *Nebraska Symposium on Motivation,* edited by M. R. Jones. Lincoln, Nebr.: University of Nebraska Press, 1960, pp. 97-141.

Unit 3
How does play promote development?

Developmental Analysis of Play Materials

Select a play material from the toys illustrated in the Appendix or from your preschool classroom. Analyze the play material by first using it yourself—explore the ways it can be used in play and think about the significance of these actions for children. Use the chart below to record your ideas.

Name of play material:

List the variety of ways the material could be used by children at play:

Considering these alternative uses, explain how the material contributes to a child's development according to the categories listed below which seem appropriate:

Physical
  gross motor

  fine motor

Social
  social interactions

  self-awareness

  sociodramatic (role playing)

61

How does play
promote development?

Developmental Analysis of
Play Materials (con't)

Emotional
    identification of emotions

    self-expression

    self-esteem

Intellectual
    language development

    perceptual skills

    creative thought processes

    concept learning

Unit 3
How does play promote development?

Sampling the Values of Play

Below are listed examples of common play materials available in most preschool centers. Look through the Play File observations for evidence of children's use of these materials. Briefly summarize the play incident, recording how the children actually played with the material, and then evaluate the developmental learning that occurred as the material was used during play.

Play Material	Play Incident	Developmental Learnings
Easel Paint		
Paste/Collage		
Clay/Play Dough		
Water		
Sand		
Woodworking		

How does play promote development?

Sampling the Values of Play (con't)

Play Material	Play Incident	Developmental Learnings
Housekeeping		
Table Games		
Blocks		
Storybooks		
Musical Instruments		
Outdoor Climber		
Tricycles		
Others		

How does play promote development?

Analysis of a Plan for Play

Plan a play activity by selecting a play material for children to use. Have the material available for children's play and evaluate the results by answering the questions below.

Describe the material you selected:

How did you expect the children to use it?

What developmental values did you see in this material to justify its selection?

How did the children actually respond?

What learnings actually occurred?

What aspects of this material made it particularly successful? Why?

What changes would you suggest for future use of the material?

Unit 3
How does play promote development?

Discussion Questions

1. Discuss the reasons why anticipating the uses and values of a play material helps a teacher expand on a child's play.

2. A parent has expressed a concern because the children "only play" in your preschool. "Children can do this at home," she states. "Why should I pay to have my child come to nursery school if all he does is play?" How would you respond?

3. You notice that Rachel consistently plays in the art area or at table games, seldom becoming involved in other areas during free play. How would you respond to this situation?

4. Why is it important for children to have fun as they play?

Unit 4

How can teachers
support play?

Objectives

1. To identify a variety of roles a teacher can use to support play.
2. To apply appropriate teacher behavior to play situations.

Components

This unit is composed of five major parts. It is suggested that they be used in the following order:

1. View MEDIAPAK 4, "How can teachers support play?" and complete the participation questions. Discuss your responses with your classmates or instructor.

2. Read Unit 4 in your text.

3. Select any supplementary reading material of interest from the suggested list (*optional*).

4. Work on the practice exercises at the conclusion of this unit:

    Analyzing Teacher Role Performance

5. Discuss the questions and issues suggested at the end of the unit.

In each part of *Planning for Play* the importance of the teacher in promoting play has been mentioned. Clearly, adults who are in contact with young children can serve a significant function in facilitating children's play.

There are many ways teachers can support play. No single suggestion will relate well to all situations or with all children. Therefore teachers should be aware of the many alternatives which can be considered and select the roles most appropriate to their particular circumstances. In addition, each teacher will think of many unique ways of applying the suggestions offered below. Such individualization in supporting play is vital toward assuring that both children and teachers are comfortable with the play atmosphere provided.

The teacher is an important part of children's play.

Information on the various ways teachers can support play is found in many sources. The theories of play discussed in Unit 1, by helping us understand the nature of play, simultaneously imply ways that play can be facilitated. Work done by play therapists such as Virginia Axline (1969) is a rich source of ideas on how to work effectively with children through the medium of play. Current research in the area of play by investigators such as Sara

Smilansky (1968) and Sylvan Krown (1974) indicates directions for teacher behaviors which most significantly affect children's play. Finally, observations and ideas gathered from teachers themselves who utilize a play approach in their curriculum development have been valuable resources.

In all these sources, several themes consistently arise regarding the types of roles that can most strongly and positively influence children's play. The roles teachers can assume can be described by the following categories:

> The teacher as
>> an observer of play
>> a reflector of play
>> an elaborator of play
>> a model of play
>> an evaluator of play
>> a planner of play

In the course of an average day, the teacher will probably find examples of ways in which each of these roles has been used to influence play. Obviously, no one single type of role behavior will satisfactorily apply to all situations. A teacher must understand the characteristics of each role and then apply the behaviors associated with these roles to appropriate play scenes.

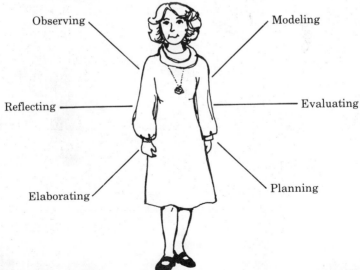

Observing   Modeling

Reflecting   Evaluating

Elaborating   Planning

A Teacher Can Support Play in Many Ways

An Observer

One of the best ways to learn how to support play most effectively is to assume the role of an observer. Observation serves as a
foundation for all the roles a teacher can use in supporting play
since it enables a teacher to gather insights into the dynamics of
children's play from the child's point of view. Although it is a
rather passive role, observation's value cannot be denied or over-
looked in favor of more active and directive types of teacher behaviors.

Observations of play can range from long, scheduled periods
over an extended period of time to spontaneous moments within
one day. Regardless of the amount of time available to a teacher,
observation should become a regular part of the day. A variety of
types of play needs to be observed to give a teacher a balanced
perspective on children's play behavior. In addition, all children
should be observed on a systematic basis. Continued effort needs
to be made to incorporate this role until it becomes almost second
nature.

An observing role provides a teacher with a wealth of information about children and play. Favorite playmates and play mater-

A teacher can learn so much by observing play!

ials, the content of popular play themes, obstacles to play, the prevalence of each level of social and object play—all are among the many areas to be observed. When a teacher is engaged in more active, participatory roles, many situations are missed or misunderstood. Since play should be focused on the child, the teacher seeking to support play should first ascertain what the children are actually doing when playing.

Before entering a child's play a teacher can gain many valuable insights by spending a few moments watching the play. Without this sensitivity the atmosphere of a play experience can be destroyed.

> Miss Miller noticed several children busily at play in the housekeeping corner. She walked over, sat in one of the chairs surrounding the small table, and asked Julee, "What are we having for dinner?" The children all paused in their play and seemed confused. Although Julee responded, "We're not having dinner. We're getting dressed to go shopping," the children's interest and enthusiasm seemed to decline.

Miss Miller's remark to Julee seemed to make the children uncomfortable with their play decision to go shopping. A few seconds of observation would have quickly informed Miss Miller of the content of the children's play. How much differently the children might have received a remark like, "Don't you look lovely for your trip to go shopping. What are you going to buy?"

The importance of observation as a teacher behavior cannot be overemphasized. Many teachers quite unfortunately feel they are not "teaching" unless they are talking to the children or otherwise actively involved in the classroom. On the contrary, a teacher who is too busy "interacting" may overlook a wealth of child behavior which, in the long run, might serve to facilitate children's play more effectively.

A Reflector

Children are eager to share the joys of their play endeavors with interested adults. Children tell adults what they are doing, ask teachers to watch them play, and show teachers the products of their play. This eagerness provides clues for another significant way teachers can support play.

The teacher as a reflector of play verbally reacts to play by simply describing what the children are doing, much like a mirror reflects our actions and expressions.

"You're painting so many blue shapes today,
John. Look how big and round this one is."

"You've spent a lot of time on this building,
Jane. It's almost as tall as you are."

"Rachel, your face has a very excited look on
it. You must have something very important
to share with us."

These verbal reflections enhance play in several ways. So often, children are not aware of the words to use when describing their play. As a reflector, a teacher builds the child's knowledge of behavior and provides a vocabulary that is meaningfully related to the child's own experiences. Secondly, reflecting a child's behavior in words informs the child of your interest in her play. This interest, in turn, builds a child's self-confidence and sense of importance so integral to the building of a positive self-concept. Thirdly, the interest and enthusiasm a teacher demonstrates when reflecting a child's play can only serve to increase the child's own enthusiasm for play. Finally, a reflective role, by demonstrating a teacher's sensitivity toward a child's activity,

"You seem to have had an accident."

seems to encourage the child to reciprocally verbalize. Children sense they have found a person who is genuinely able to understand them. Like all humans, children respond eagerly to such a person.

A reflective role, because it merely mirrors back the child's own actions, feelings, or activities, does not interfere with the child's control over play. Thus, the behavior can remain on a high level of playfulness according to the criteria discussed in Unit 1. Children continue and even expand on their play, using the reflective teacher as an appreciative audience.

An Elaborator

The role of an elaborator of play flows easily from a reflective role. As an elaborator, a teacher identifies the child's play activity and supplements the behavior with additional ideas, materials, or information that might expand the play. It remains up to the child whether to incorporate the teacher's suggestions, as well as just how this might be done. However, the teacher extends the play from an initial level of behavior to a newer and related level with this elaborative input.

> "Thank you for showing me your beautiful car, Aaron. It's wheels really turn, don't they. I think it would be fun to build a road for your car over in the block area. Maybe Ronnie can help you."

> "You firefighters are certainly busy today. Here is some rope I had in the closet—you can use it for hoses to put out the fires."

> "I see Brad is rolling his clay into a long shape. Can you think of some other shapes you can make your clay into?"

As children try the suggestions offered by the teacher they not only extend their play to new levels but also are encouraged to make up their own elaborations.

The specific method for introducing an elaborative idea is important. A simple, positive statement, as illustrated in earlier examples, is usually more well received. A common but generally unsuccessful method is to phrase an elaborative comment as a question. The all-time loser is, of course, the "would you like to ..." query. Polite as it seems, often the response is an abrupt "no."

This negative response often does not truly indicate a refusal as much as it does an uncertainty on the child's part, perhaps because she has never tried something before or because she feels she is being forced into something she may not enjoy. Once again, the importance of the child's sense of control over play is very important. A positive statement still leaves the child free to decide, but the nature of the elaboration sounds far more appealing.

A Model

Teachers are significant figures to young children and thereby serve as important models of behavior. This fact enables teachers to help children play by means of actually entering a play scene as a player. Children can observe and then imitate the teacher's behavior, later expanding on their imitations in play. Examples of modeling roles are demonstrated in Smilansky's research on sociodramatic play (1968). Teachers in one group got children involved in play by actually participating in sociodramatic play sequences themselves. The findings showed that children with teachers who modeled sociodramatic play began to assume similar play behaviors of their own accord.

Children enjoy teachers who join in their play.

Most early childhood educators have discouraged teachers from entering into play by providing models. The classic example is art: if a teacher participates in playing with clay, for example, the child will avoid making her own creations. This danger of the modeling role must be recognized; its applicability may be limited to certain types of situations and to children who already have strong play skills.

It is often taken for granted that all children know how to play by virtue of the fact that they are children. This is apparently not true; many children do not have the physical materials, the social experiences, the language competencies, or the knowledge background needed to support prolonged play episodes. The modeling efforts of teachers can effect changes in children's play more quickly than previously mentioned reflective and elaborative roles. Once children begin to experience success in play, they will soon demonstrate initiative in planning their own play experiences. At this time the teacher may effectively move to less directive roles.

A modeling role is also appropriate for situations where a particular skill or technique is necessary for safety or proper use of equipment. At carpentry, for example, a teacher would want to clearly demonstrate how a hammer or saw is to be used. Similarly, situations where certain techniques may help a child achieve a desired result may be appropriate times for modeling. When easel painting, a child who is experiencing difficulty because the brush is being held in an awkward position may benefit from being shown another way to hold it.

In situations such as dramatic play, where a teacher enters as a fellow player, modeling may serve a different purpose than technique instruction. As a fellow player, the teacher adds a measure of legitimacy to the play behavior—she implies that it is okay to play. This type of encouragement can reinforce the child's interest in future play involvement. A teacher can avoid the tendency for children to assume a passive audience role to his play by maintaining a model role in which he participates in play as an equal to children. By consistently involving the children in the play process, the teacher can soon move from a modeling role to more supplementary roles.

An Evaluator

The teacher needs to be concerned with the effectiveness of efforts to support play among children. The best measure of the

success of a teacher's role performance can be the performance of
children. Therefore, teachers also assume an evaluator role in
analyzing play. Three major areas have been identified as being
of particular concern:

1. The degree of playfulness of behavior among children (Who?
   Why? What?).
2. The type of play evidenced in social and object play.
3. The developmental gains made by children who have been
   actively involved in a play curriculum.

If teachers have been successful in supporting play, children
will score highly on the extent of their playfulness. They will move
through a variety of social and object play levels and demonstrate
competence in their play according to their developmental age.
Children will also learn from their play and exhibit increasing
gains in all developmental areas.

Teachers who cannot find such evidences of success in children's play can then begin to locate the area or areas of weakness.
Perhaps the children have not been given ample control over the
direction of their play and therefore have not experienced adequate playlike situations. Perhaps the types of materials available
do not support symbolic forms of play at sufficient levels, or the
content areas are not relevant to the children's own experiences.
Once the weakness has been identified, the teacher can then use
the various roles of observing, reflecting, elaborating, and modeling to further strive to support play.

A Planner

Finally, a fundamental role of a teacher is that of a planner of
play. Each of the roles discussed earlier incorporates some form of
planning on the part of a teacher to support play most effectively.
In addition, a planning role utilizes the information gathered in
all the other role functions a teacher may perform. Thus, planning
has a particularly significant role in supporting play.

The planning process involves gathering information through
observation and interaction with children and using this information to select appropriate play experiences which will extend and
support play. Planning provides a dynamic structure underlying
children's play. Often, however, planning efforts are subtle and

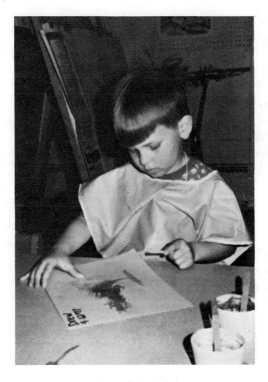

Planning a special art activity can promote play.

unnoticed—a teacher simply comments "What bright colors you are using" while observing a child engrossed in easel painting or decides to place some dramatic play props out for a grocery store scene. While planning may be a relatively "quiet" role for the teacher, its impact is significant; much of the teacher's success in supporting play is dependent on the effectiveness of planning.

Conclusion

Play, in its fullest extent, is a spontaneous and child-centered form of behavior. Nevertheless, the teacher can play an important function in supporting play. Several different types of roles are appropriate to the support of play; teachers who are aware of the qualities of these various roles and who try to develop competencies within each of them will better facilitate the play of children around them.

How can a teacher support play in this situation?

REFERENCES

Axline, V. *Play Therapy.* New York: Ballantine Books, 1969.

Krown, S. *Three and Fours Go to School.* Englewood Cliffs, N.J.: Prentice-Hall, 1974.

Smilansky, S. *The Effects of Socio-dramatic Play on Disadvantaged Preschool Children.* New York: Appleton-Century-Crofts, 1968.

How can teachers support play?

Analyzing Teacher Role Performance

Using your Play File observations, look for examples of various types of roles teachers used to support the play of children. Describe what happened in column B (providing information on both teacher and child behavior) and analyze the effectiveness of the teacher's role performance in column C—how well play was supported.

A Role	B Teacher Behavior — Child Behavior	C Effectiveness of Role
Observer		
Reflector		
Elaborator		

How can teachers support play?

Analyzing Teacher Role Performance (con't)

A Role	B Teacher Behavior — Child Behavior	C Effectiveness of Role
Model		
Evaluator		
Planner		

Unit 4
How can teachers support play?

Discussion Questions

1. Discuss several reasons why it is important for teachers to develop competencies in supporting play through a variety of role forms.

2. What signs might indicate that a teacher is assuming too directive a role in supporting children's play?

Suggested Readings

Almy, M., ed. *Early Childhood Play: Selected Readings Related to Cognition and Motivation*. New York: Academic Press, 1968.

Ashton-Warner, S. *Teacher*. New York: Simon and Schuster, 1963.

Biber, B., Shapiro, E., and Wickens, D. *Promoting Cognitive Growth: A Developmental-Interaction Point of View*. Washington, D.C.: National Association for the Education of Young Children, 1970.

Bruner, J. S., Jolly, A., and Sylva, K. *Play: Its Role in Development and Evolution*. New York: Basic Books, 1976.

Caplan, F., and Caplan, T. *The Power of Play*. New York: Anchor Press, 1974.

Cass, J. *The Significance of Children's Play*. London: B. T. Blatsford, 1971.

Curry, N., and Arnaud, S., eds. *Play: The Child Strives Toward Self-Realization*. Washington, D.C.: National Association for the Education of Young Children, 1971.

Ellis, M. *Why People Play*. Englewood Cliffs, N.J.: Prentice-Hall, 1973.

Erikson, E. "Toys and Reasons." In *Childhood and Society,* pp. 209-47. New York: W. W. Norton, 1963.

Flavell, J. H. *The Developmental Psychology of Jean Piaget*. New York: Van Nostrand, 1963.

Gesell, A. *The Infant and Child in the Culture of Today*. New York: Harper and Row, 1943.

Gordon, I. *Child Learning Through Child Play*. New York: St. Martin's Press, 1970.

Hartley, R. E., Frank, L. K., and Goldenson, R. M. *Understanding Children's Play*. New York: Columbia University Press, 1952.

Herron, R. E., and Sutton-Smith, B., eds. *Child's Play*. New York: John Wiley, 1971.

Issacs, S. *Intellectual Growth in Children*. New York: Schocken Books, 1966.

Issacs, S. *Social Development in Children*. New York: Schocken Books, 1972.

Millar, S. *The Psychology of Play*. Baltimore, Md.: Penguin Books, 1968.

Murphy, L. *The Widening World of Childhood*. New York: Basic Books, 1962.

Piers, M. *Play and Development*. New York: W. W. Norton, 1972.

Sponseller, D., ed. *Play: A Learning Medium*. Washington, D.C.: National Association for the Education of Young Children, 1974.

Appendix

Samples of Play Materials

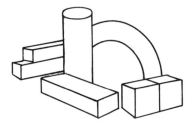

Unit Blocks

Dress-up Hat

Ball

Crayons

Puzzle

Truck

85

Play File Observation Form

Record your observations of children's play during a time period of approximately five to fifteen minutes. Be descriptive and objective when recording your observations.

Observer's Name: __Jill Stevens_____ *Date:* __Oct. 10, 1978__

Children's Names and Ages: *Name:*__Chris_____ *Age:*__3 yr. 9 mo.__
*Name:*__Glen_____ *Age:*__4 yr. 1 mo.__
*Name:*__Jane_____ *Age:*__4 yr. 7 mo.__
*Name:*_____ *Age:*_____

Setting:

Beginning of day. Free play period.

Observation Notes

Chris enters the room smiling and says, "Look at my new shirt, teacher!"

"It's a special Sesame Street shirt, isn't it?"

"Uh-huh."

Chris notices the rocking boat which has been placed in the block area today. He walks directly to it. Glen is already sitting in the boat. Chris asks, "Can I come in?" Glen nods his head "yes" and Chris climbs in. They rock back and forth trying to get the boat to rock higher and higher, laughing as they rock. This continues for three minutes until Chris sees Jane at the art table. He shouts "Stop" to Glen and jumps out of the boat.

Chris sits next to Jane at the art table where collage materials have been set out. Chris says "Hi" to Jane and both begin to work. Chris carefully squeezes the glue on the paper, using back and forth motions until almost the entire page is covered. He glances occasionally at what Jane is doing but continues with his own work. Now he starts to select collage materials to place on his paste. It's a fall theme, and Chris selects only the large, colorful leaves to glue on his paper. Jane has finished her collage and even though Chris is still working on his, he tells the teacher, "I'm finished too." Both Chris and Jane leave the art table.

Play File Observation Form

Observer's Name: _____ Date: _____

Children's Names and Ages: Name: _____ Age: ____

Name: _____ Age: ____

Name: _____ Age: ____

Name: _____ Age: ____

Setting:

Observation Notes

Play File Observation Form

Observer's Name: _____ *Date:* _____

Children's Names and Ages: *Name:* _____ *Age:* ____

Name: _____ *Age:* ____

Name: _____ *Age:* ____

Name: _____ *Age:* ____

Setting:

Observation Notes

Play File Observation Form

Observer's Name: ———————————————— *Date:* ————

Children's Names and Ages: *Name:* ———————— *Age:* ———

Name: ———————— *Age:* ———

Name: ———————— *Age:* ———

Name: ———————— *Age:* ———

Setting:

Observation Notes

Play File Observation Form

Observer's Name: _____ *Date:* _____

Children's Names and Ages: Name: _____ *Age:* ____

Name: _____ *Age:* ____

Name: _____ *Age:* ____

Name: _____ *Age:* ____

Setting:

Observation Notes

Play File Observation Form

Observer's Name: _____ *Date:* _____

Children's Names and Ages: Name: _____ *Age:* ____

Name: _____ *Age:* ____

Name: _____ *Age:* ____

Name: _____ *Age:* ____

Setting:

Observation Notes

Play File Observation Form

Observer's Name: _____ *Date:* _____

Children's Names and Ages: Name: _____ *Age:* _____

Name: _____ *Age:* _____

Name: _____ *Age:* _____

Name: _____ *Age:* _____

Setting:

Observation Notes

Play File Observation Form

Observer's Name: _____ *Date:* _____

Children's Names and Ages: Name: _____ *Age:* _____

Name: _____ *Age:* _____

Name: _____ *Age:* _____

Name: _____ *Age:* _____

Setting:

Observation Notes

Predictive Observation Form

Play File Observation Form

Observer's Name: _____ *Date:* _____

Children's Names and Ages: Name: _____ *Age:* ____

Name: _____ *Age:* ____

Name: _____ *Age:* ____

Name: _____ *Age:* ____

Setting:

Observation Notes

Play File Observation Form

Observer's Name: _____ *Date:* _____

Children's Names and Ages: Name: _____ *Age:* ____

Name: _____ *Age:* ____

Name: _____ *Age:* ____

Name: _____ *Age:* ____

Setting:

Observation Notes

Play File Observation Form

Observer's Name: _____ *Date:* _____

Children's Names and Ages: Name: _____ *Age:* _____

Name: _____ *Age:* _____

Name: _____ *Age:* _____

Name: _____ *Age:* _____

Setting:

Observation Notes

Fire Observation Form

Play File Observation Form

Observer's Name: _____ *Date:* _____

Children's Names and Ages: Name: _____ *Age:* _____

Name: _____ *Age:* _____

Name: _____ *Age:* _____

Name: _____ *Age:* _____

Setting:

Observation Notes

Play File Observation Form

Observer's Name: _____ *Date:* _____

Children's Names and Ages: *Name:* _____ *Age:* ____

Name: _____ *Age:* ____

Name: _____ *Age:* ____

Name: _____ *Age:* ____

Setting:

Observation Notes

Play File Observation Form

Observer's Name: _____ *Date:* _____

Children's Names and Ages: Name: _____ *Age:* _____

Name: _____ *Age:* _____

Name: _____ *Age:* _____

Name: _____ *Age:* _____

Setting:

Observation Notes

Play File Observation Form

Observer's Name: _____ *Date:* _____

Children's Names and Ages: Name: _____ *Age:* _____

Name: _____ *Age:* _____

Name: _____ *Age:* _____

Name: _____ *Age:* _____

Setting:

Observation Notes